A Note to Parents and Teachers

DK READERS is a compelling reading programme for children. The programme is designed in conjunction with leading literacy experts, including Cliff Moon M.Ed., who has spent many years as a teacher and teacher educator specializing in reading. Cliff Moon has written more than 160 books for children and teachers. He is series editor to Collins Big Cat.

Beautiful illustrations and superb full-colour photographs combine with engaging, easy-to-read stories to offer a fresh approach to each subject in the series. Each DK READER is guaranteed to capture a child's interest while developing his or her reading skills, general knowledge, and love of reading.

The five levels of DK READERS are aimed at different reading abilities, enabling you to choose the books that are exactly right for your child:

Pre-level 1: Learning to read
Level 1: Beginning to read
Level 2: Beginning to read alone
Level 3: Reading alone
Level 4: Proficient readers

The "normal" age at which a child begins to read can be anywhere from three to eight years old. Adult participation through the lower levels is very helpful for providing encouragement, discussing storylines and sounding out unfamiliar words.

No matter which level you select, you can be sure that you are helping your child learn to read, then read to learn!

LONDON, NEW YORK, MUNICH,
MELBOURNE, AND DELHI

DK LONDON
Series Editor Deborah Lock
Art Director Martin Wilson
Production Editor Francesca Wardell
Jacket Designer Martin Wilson

Reading Consultant
Cliff Moon, M.Ed.

DK DELHI
Senior Editor Priyanka Nath
Senior Art Editor Rajnish Kashyap
Assistant Editor Deeksha Saikia
Assistant Designer Tanvi Sahu
DTP Designer Anita Yadav
Picture Researcher Sumedha Chopra

First published in Great Britain by
Dorling Kindersley Limited
80 Strand, London, WC2R 0RL

Copyright © 2013 Dorling Kindersley Limited
A Penguin Company

10 9 8 7 6 5 4 3 2 1
001—187464—June/2013

A CIP catalogue record for this book
is available from the British Library
ISBN: 978-1-40932-659-5

Colour reproduction by Colourscan, Singapore
Printed and bound in China by L Rex Printing Co., Ltd.

The publisher would like to thank the following for their kind
permission to reproduce their photographs:
a=above, b=below/bottom, c=centre, l=left, r=right, t=top

4 Getty Images: Jetta Productions / Iconica (b). **5 Corbis:** Dave Blackey / All
Canada Photos. **6 Corbis:** Federico Gambarini / dpa (bl). **Dreamstime.com:**
Anhong (br). **7 Getty Images:** Dieter Spears / Photodisc (bl). **8-9 Alamy Images:**
Wally Bauman Photo. **8 Dreamstime.com:** Jaypetersen (br). **9 Corbis:** Ken
Davies (br). **Dreamstime.com:** Blaze86 (bl). **10-11 Alamy Images:** Manfred Bail
/ imagebroker. **11 Alamy Images:** format4 (br); Andrew Rubtsov (t). **Getty
Images:** Thinkstock / Comstock Images (bl). **12-13 Corbis:** Nick Rains. **12
Dreamstime.com:** David Gaylor (bl). **13 Dreamstime.com:** Michael Shake (bc);
Thyrymn (br). **Shutterstock:** (bl). **14-15 Dreamstime.com:** Stangot. **14
Dreamstime.com:** Stepan Olenych (bl, br). **15 Dreamstime.com:** Stepan
Olenych (bl); Steirus (br). **16 Dreamstime.com:** Rui Matos (bl); Philippa Willitts
(br). **Getty Images:** Bloomberg (c). **17 Corbis:** HBSS. **Dreamstime.com:** Artzzz
(bl); Christian Lagereek (bc). **Getty Images:** Stockbyte (br). **18-19 Dreamstime.
com:** Picstudio. **19 Dreamstime.com:** Grafvision (br); Photobac (bl). **Fotolia:**
skampixel (tr). **Getty Images:** Vasiliki Varvaki / Photodisc (bc). **20 Dreamstime.
com:** Dmitry Kalinovsky (bl). **21 Dreamstime.com:** Dmitry Kalinovsky (bc).
22-23 Corbis: Naljah Feanny. **23 Dreamstime.com:** Mlan61 (bl). **24-25 Getty
Images:** John Macdougall / AFP. **24 Dreamstime.com:** Reinhardt (bl). **25
Dreamstime.com:** Bjorn Heller (bc); Dmitri Melnik (br). **26-27 Corbis:**
moodboard. **26 Dreamstime.com:** Dtfoxfoto (bl). **Getty Images:** Universal
Images Group (br). **27 Dreamstime.com:** Ralf Broskvar (bc, tr); Robert Pernell
(bl). **Getty Images:** Robert Llewellyn / Workbook Stock (br). **28-29 Alamy
Images:** Marvin Dembinsky Photo Associates. **28 Dreamstime.com:** Robwilson39
(br). **29 Dorling Kindersley:** Aberdeen Fire Department, Maryland (bl).
Dreamstime.com: Robwilson39 (bc); Charles Vazquez (br). **30-31 Corbis:** Alan
Ashley / NewSport. **30 Corbis:** Car Culture (br). **31 Dreamstime.com:** Gorgios
(bc); **Gunter Nezhoda** (bl). **33 Corbis:** Federico Gambarini / dpa (br)

Jacket images: *Front:* **Corbis:** Mark Karrass

All other images © Dorling Kindersley
For further information see: www.dkimages.com

Discover more at
www.dk.com

Contents

DK READERS

LEARNING pre-level **1** TO READ

Big Trucks

A Dorling Kindersley Book

Trucks are BIG.

Trucks are long.

Trucks carry
heavy things.

Trucks carry loads along the roads.

load

trucks

cab

Flatbed trucks carry loads on their trailers.

trailer

flatbed trucks

load

Breakdown trucks carry broken down cars.

boom ————

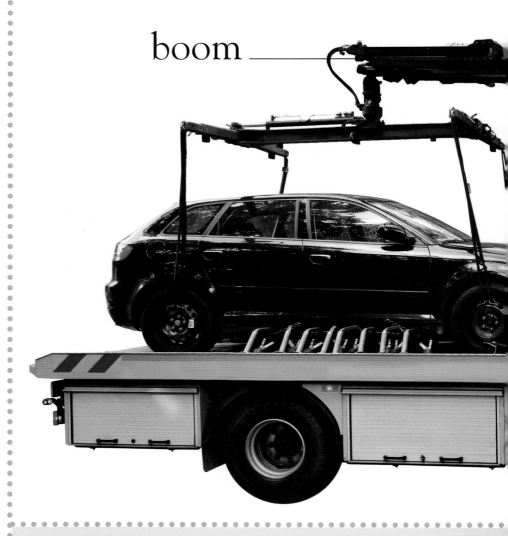

exhaust

giant trucks

Giant trucks pull
many trailers
on long trips.

trailer

Road rollers flatten the road.

road rollers

drum roller

Forklift trucks move heavy loads.

load

 forklift trucks

driver

fork

Diggers lift rubble in their buckets.

bucket

diggers

rubble

Wheeled loaders scoop up large rocks.

wheeled loaders

bucket

rock

Dumper trucks tip to let the rubble slide out.

rubble

dumper trucks

cab

Excavators dig trenches with their shovels.

excavators

shovel

trench

Compactors press down with their spiked wheels.

compactors

spiked
wheel

Fire engines have hoses and ladders for putting out fires.

ladder _____.

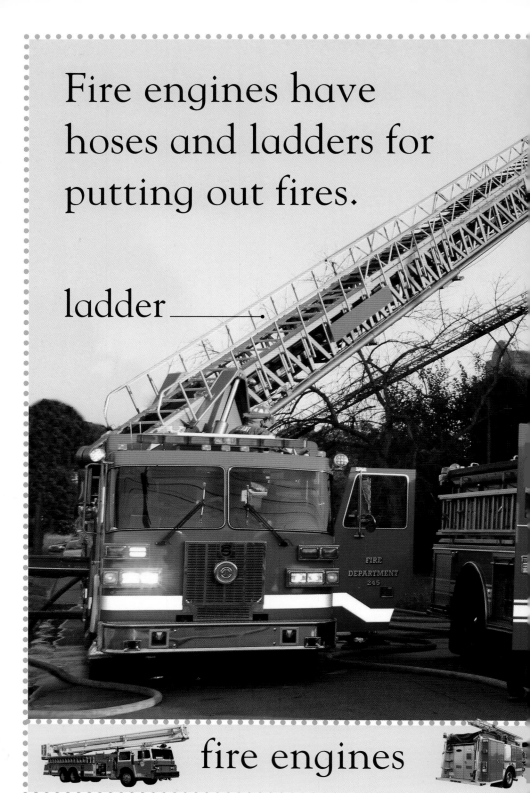

fire engines

_____ hose

Monster trucks do stunts on their huge wheels.

monster trucks

wheel

Glossary

Compactor
a machine that squashes waste or soil into smaller amounts

Excavator
a machine that has a cab and bucket on a turning platform

Forklift truck
a truck that lifts and moves loads

Monster truck
a pickup truck with very large wheels for doing stunts

Wheeled loader
a machine with a bucket to dig out earth and rocks